MAHATMA GANDHI ON ETHICS

About the Author

Dr. Anil Dutta Mishra (*b.* 1965) started his career as an Assistant Professor in the Department of Non-violence and Peace Studies, Jain Vishva Bharati University, Ladnun, Rajasthan. His area of specialization includes Public Administration, Grass-root Politics, Gender Issues, Ecology and Human Rights.

Besides a number of research papers in leading professional journals, he has to his credit 16 books including *Problems and Prospects of Working Women in Urban India* (1994); *Fundamentals of Gandhism* (1995); *Gandhian Approach to Contemporary Problems* (1996); *Decentralized Planning in India : A Study of Objectives and Operational Framework* (1999); *Gender Perspectives : Participation, Empowerment and Development* (1999); *Perspectives on Human Rights* (2002); *Rediscovering Gandhi* (2002); *Patterns of Gender Violence* (2002); *Challenges of Twenty First Century and Gandhian Alternative* (2003); *India and Canada; Past, Present and Future* (2003); *Public Governance and Decentralization : Essays in Honour of T.N. Chaturvedi* (2003); *Gandhian Alternative to Contemporary Problems* (2004); *Globalization Myth and Reality* (2004); *Gandhian Alternative* Vol. III, *Socio-Political Thought* (2005); *Inspiring Thoughts of Mahatma Gandhi* (2008); and *Terrorism : A Global Challenge* (2009).

Mahatma Gandhi on Ethics

Anil Dutta Mishra

CONCEPT PUBLISHING COMPANY PVT. LTD.,
NEW DELHI-110 059

ISBN-13 : 978-81-8069-681-7

First Published 2010

Published and Printed by

Concept
Since 1974

Concept Publishing Company Pvt. Ltd.
Regd. Office :
A/15-16, Commercial Block, Mohan Garden
New Delhi-110059 (India)
Phones : 25351460, 25351794, *Fax* : 091-11-25357109
Email : publishing@conceptpub.com
Website : www.conceptpub.com

Editorial Office :
H-13, Bali Nagar, New Delhi-110 015, India.

Cataloging in Publication Data-- *Courtesy:* D.K. Agencies (P) Ltd. <docinfo@dkagencies.com>

Mishra, A. D. (Anil Dutta), 1965-
Mahatma Gandhi on ethics / Anil Dutta Mishra.
p. cm.
Includes bibliographical references.
Includes index.
ISBN 13: 9788180696817

1. Gandhi, Mahatma, 1869-1948--Ethics. I. Title.

DDC 170.92 22

Dedicated to

Shri T.N. Chaturvedi, former Governor and Member of Parliament for his honesty, integrity and prestive purity in private and public life.

Preface

Gandhi's life was an open book. He made himself brick by brick and step by step. He reached the top where even the saints rarely reach. He combined facts with value, theory with practice, body with soul. He conducted experiments after experiments to achieve the final goal. His entire public life was based on ethics, morality, voluntary poverty, simplicity and pristine purity. He accepted positive points from Western and Eastern tradition. He read and accepted the noble points from all world religions. He was aware of what is going on in the world around and with latest technique and scientific enquiry. Even though for Gandhi, *Gita* was a source book. Like Aurobindo, Tilak and many others, Gandhi got ultimate strength and inspiration from *Gita* which is the gist of all *Vedas.* He made title of his Autobiography as *An Autobiography : My Experiments With Truth.* From early childhood he was truthful. He never bowed his head. He always upheld the self-esteem and dignity of human being. He was firm in his conviction. And on the basis of Non-violence, *Satyagraha, Swadesi* and *Swaraj* he laid the freedom struggle of India and showed the way to the world.

Gandhi's approach was human centric. He wrote and spoke on all aspects of life. After going through the *Collected Works of Mahatma Gandhi* (CWMG) word by word, I came to the conclusion that even whole life is not enough to understand Mahatma Gandhi. For that, one has to be born and reborn again and again.

To work on "Gandhi on Ethics " is a Himalayan task. I took it as a challenge and started working on the subject. In the beginning, there was lot of problems due to vastness of the available literature on Gandhi. These collections constitute the written and spoken words of Mahatma Gandhi reflecting, in volume after volume, the mood and temper of the times and illuminating every aspect of India's political, social, economic and spiritual history and aspirations. Even in the era of Globalization, particularly after economic crises all over the world, one is debating about various approaches to development. One can draw inspiration from Mahatma Gandhi's words and deeds which lead us to a harmonious whole between urban and rural, materialism and spiritualism, theory and practice, localism and globalism, ethical and unethical, pain and pleasure, love and hate, secularism and communalism, development and environment, and war and peace. This is the most appropriate time when one can realize Mahatma Gandhi's view. Today they are more relevant than ever before or even when he was alive.

To work on any of the concepts of Mahatma Gandhi and its formulation is not an easy task. Collecting and researching materials on Ethics from Gandhiji's writings, speeches and letters, representing his sixty years of very active public life was no easy task. To locate specific material from the *Collected Works of Mahatma Gandhi, Young India, Harijan, Navajivan,* D.G. Tendulkar etc. is also very difficult. It needs thorough and deep understanding of Gandhi by the researcher.

Gandhi is now, part of history and his words belong to humanity. There is vast literature on Gandhi, apart from his original works or compilation of his works, popularly known as *CWMG*, which are hundred bulky volumes. The ethical concepts of Mahatma Gandhi as reflected through his writings and speeches are scattered. These scattered materials were collected, classified and put in one place by using only the primary source.

I have dealt with most of the significant issues of the theme. Yet due to the pervasive vastness of the theme and constraints of time and space, some gaps, misunderstandings and overlapping—unavoidable in this venture—have remained despite best intentions and efforts. I am conscious of these due to the nature and complexity of Gandhian Thought. Whether I have succeeded in the endeavour only time will tell. While presenting the material at one place to the general readers, researchers and scholars, I hope, despite of its many shortcomings they will consider the work on the subject useful and worth my effort. I am sure and hopeful that the work will be worthwhile contribution on the subject with its immense current and future significance not only for Indian politicians and public servants but also for others.

In part one, an attempt has been made to present a framework of Gandhian ethics keeping the Gandhian ethos in mind. In part two, original Ethical Religion by M.K. Gandhi is placed for the reader's deeper understanding of the subject.

This work has been done in the most odd, depressing and frustrating environment. Without God's grace and reading *Gita,* this work would not have been completed. I have no words to thank God. *Gita* showed the way and gave me inner strength to fight against unGandhian activities in Gandhian Institutions. Whether I did right or wrong, only the time and God alone will judge.

Last but not the least, I am grateful to those who stand behind me.

Anil Dutta Mishra

Contents

PART ONE

ETHICS : A CONCEPTUAL FRAMEWORK

1

Ethics : A Conceptual Framework

I

Ethics is a widely used term. One of the upshots of such wide usage of the term is the diverse ways in which it has been looked at. Viewed broadly, ethics and morals have been used interchangeably. The rationale of such use is that both the terms have been derived etymologically from Latin and Greek words with the same meaning. It has also been understood that to define ethics one needs first to talk about morality and values. Morality is concerned with those practices and activities that are considered right or wrong, it is also concerned with the values those practices reflect and the rules through which they are carried out within a given setting. Morality in effect, includes a number of values, that are reflected in laws, rules and regulations or in policies or procedures. Value comprise a moral flavour in the sense that they carry an individual's ideas as to what is right, good or desirable. Values, to a large extent, would be an individual's notions about morality and ethics. In other words, values, morality and ethics are interrelated and cannot be understood in isolation of one another.

Encyclopedia of Social Sciences defines ethics as "the organization or criticism of conduct in terms of notions like good, right or welfare...Ethics is the secular and critical manner of taking account of the rationalizing process in conduct. Its temper is non-mystical, and its orientation is social rather than theological". The New Encyclopedia Britannica defines ethics as "the branch of philosophy that is concerned with what is morally good and bad, right and wrong; a synonym for it is moral philosophy. Traditionally, ethics has undertaken to analyze, evaluate, and develop normative moral criteria for dealing with moral problems…". "Ethics" and "ethical" are often used synonymously with "morals" (or morality) and "moral", as when reference is made indifferently to the ethics or to the morality of a person or a group, to their ethical or moral virtues or qualities. The Oxford English Dictionary defines ethics as the science of morals or moral principles. It is very often used as a synonym or even an interchangeable expression for term like values, norms, standards, morality etc. The word 'ethics' is defined as "the discipline dealing with what is good and bad and with normal duty and obligations". Thus, personal ethics has been referred to as "the rules by which an individual lives his or her personal life", and accounting ethics pertains to "the code that guides the professional conduct" of persons engaged in various activities. Business ethics is concerned with truth and justice and has a variety of aspects : market, society, corporate behaviour *et al.* All the three types of ethics are interrelated and that each is the manifestation of other in Gandhian perspective.

Ethics cannot be shaped and sustained in isolation. The heuristic process requires a supportive environment in which public opinion plays a significant part. In every field of activity, the components of ethical conduct have to be identified and its dynamics worked out. Efficiency, economy, effectiveness, equity and equality of treatment, transparency, purity, neutral, and excellence, among others, are deemed to be commonly the ingredients essential to the conduct of public life. Ethics in more general terms deals with moral duty and obligation. Thus, ethics becomes a tool for searching moral standards. The utility of ethics rests on the fact that it requires one to reason, to analyse and to search for morally correct position while taking a decision or pursuing a particular course of action. Ethics, as an academic area, is a branch of philosophy. The philosophers have studied and argued about ethics for centuries. But our concern here is to relate the term ethics particularly in the context of Gandhi. Ethics in Gandhian paradigm has no narrow religious, sectarian or creedal implications. Ethics is something like electricity, not apparent to the naked eye, but felt instantaneously in specific conditions and visible when power is switched on. It has something to do with the sense of right and wrong—what is permissible, what is not done. Ethics has several attributes, some of which are universalistic in nature, while others are also bound by time and place. It may be specific to a particular task situation, profession or area of responsibility. Certain things are expected from everyone while there may be a few specific things expected according to the nature of groups or responsibilities. Ethics is something related to a state of mind, or a way of looking at things which may develop into a pattern of behaviour or way of life and social conduct. One's values may indicate or reveal one's preferences, which norms identify social prescriptions or obligations which have a regulatory significance.

In the present era there is a shift as there is a change in ethics, from what Max Weber called the Protestant ethics to what Wayne A.R. Leys calls the social ethics. The protestant ethics emphasized the quest for individual salvation through individual efforts, thrift and competitive forces. The social ethics emphasized that moral good is determined by pressures of society against the individual.

Gandhian ethics is much more than Protestant ethics and social ethics. For Gandhi there is no watertight compartment between personal/private/social ethics. For Gandhi, *dharma* is everything. His ethics is guided by what Lord Krishna in *Bhagvad Gita* [Chapter III, Verse 20] enunciated several thousand years ago *i.e. "Loka samgrahamevapi sampasyankar tumarhasi"*. Gandhi set an example of self-sacrifice, demonstrated the highest standards of personal integrity, honesty, pristine purity, transparent public and private life, fairness and justice which are the basic ingredients of Gandhi's ethics. *Dharma,* in the Indian tradition, commands morality in the sense of righteous conduct. Mahatma Gandhi has raised *dharma* to a higher pedestal, signifying a quality through which we know "our duty in human life and our relation with other selves".

Chester I. Bernard characterizes moral behaviour or ethical conduct as "governed by beliefs or feelings of what is right or wrong, regardless of self-interests or immediate consequence of a decision to do or not to do specific things under particular condition. Ethical behaviour/conduct is partly a matter of civilization, legacy, family inheritance, a fallout of personal philosophy but, is certainly a social imperative if the society is to have an equilibrium conducive to social cohesiveness and good life. In the social perspective, it does become for an individual, at times, a matter of conscience or 'inner voice' as Mahatma Gandhi called it. Ethical conduct has wider and positive dimensions. Only four days before his assassination Mahatma Gandhi thus warned the country during his prayer meeting : "The subject of corruption referred to by the correspondent is not new. Only it has become much worse than before. Restraint from without has practically gone. Corruption will go when the large number of persons given to the unworthy practice realize that the nation does not exist for them but they do for the nation. It requires a high code of morals, extreme vigilance on the part of those who are free from the corrupt practice and who have influence over corrupt servants. Indifference in such matters is criminal. If our evening prayers are genuine, they must play no mean part in removing from our midst the demon of corruption.[1] Unfortunately the warning went unheeded. This is the matter for soul-searching.

Ethics can generally be defined as the realization of the need to justify one's life and the decision to be ethical entails the choice of a particular value : "the sense of satisfaction derived from knowing that one may judge his own life as he would judge another's and find it good". This requires some critical self-analysis and for Gandhi the quest for Truth largely depended upon the truth about the self. When Gandhi claimed that an individual's "highest duty in life is to serve mankind and take his share in bettering its condition", he added that this could not be done unless and until one understands and respects the self. True morality, that is, life based on following ethical rules, then, for Gandhi, consists not in conformity but in discovering the subjectively true path and in fearlessly following it :

> It is noble voluntarily to do what is good and right. The true sign of man's nobility is the fact that, instead of being driven about like a cloud before the wind, he stands firm and can do, and in fact does, what he deems proper.

'True morality' had to be grounded in religion—it had to be a living creed than a policy of expedience. He

1. M.K. Gandhi, *Delhi Diary*, 26.1.1948.

included the non-orthodox religion in his definition by explaining that this in fact meant that "morality should be observed as a religion". The "highest form of morality" in Gandhi's ethical system is the practice of altruism/self-sacrificing. For Gandhi it was never enough that an individual merely avoided causing evil; they had to actively promote good and actively prevent evil. In conflict situation it can be difficult to remember to forsake possible satisfaction by the active prevention of evil to the opponent by working for the good of all parties. The question of why one should act in a moral way has occupied much time in the history of philosophical inquiry. Gandhi's answer to this is that happiness, religion and wealth depend upon sincerity to the self, an absence of malice towards and exploitation of, others, and always acting "with a pure mind". Gandhi's ethics, therefore, stems not from the intellectual deductive formula. "Do unto others as you would have been them unto you".

Gandhi restricted himself to issues of *dharma*—which the Gujarati original defines as "morality practiced for the sake of the *atman*"—which even a child could understand, hoping that, if he could present the story objectively and in a spirit of humility, it might help other seekers. Gandhi's concept of *dharma* was the result of many influences. Rapt listening to the *Ramayana,* the eager enjoyment of mythological stories of devotion to truth and service of parents, the observance of vows and visits to temples of both the Vaishnava and Saiva sects were not less important than the later study of Ruskin and Tolstoy and the *Sermon on the Mount* in moulding his heart and forming his outlook. In the *Autobiography* too, as in communion of saints described by Tulsidas, we watch a moving Prayag, the confluence of three streams, the Jamuna of *karma,* the Ganga of *bhakti* and Saraswati of *jnana.* This view of *dharma,* linking action and experience, morality and religion, embraced politics too, as part of an incessant war against evil in society. In an article in *Young India* dated 12.5.1920, Gandhiji claims to be neither a saint nor a politician, but a humble seeker after truth making experiments about some of the eternal relative of life. Gandhi, who was familiar with the Jain doctrine of *anekantavada,* the many-sidedness of truth, recognized that "every case can be seen from no less than seven points of view, all of which are probably correct by themselves, but not correct at the same time and in the same circumstances". The *Autobiography* provides humorous illustrations of this absence of dogmatism in Gandhi's comments on his own actions.

Gandhi had not used the word ethics in the sense as we understand in Social Sciences. When we work on Gandhi we have to follow the path shown not by others but Gandhi himself. Here I would like to quote Gandhi : "my aim is not to be consistent with my previous statements on a given question, but to be consistent with truth, as it may present itself to me at a given moment. The result has been that I have grown from truth to truth. I have saved my memory an undue strain; and what is more, whenever I have been obliged to compare my writings even of fifty years ago with the latest, I have discovered no inconsistency will do to take the meaning that my latest writings may yield unless, of course, they prefer the old".

Further, one should make the point clear. To regard Gandhi as a philosopher or system builder or ethicist, in the academic or professional or Western sense, will be a great mistake. He was a practical man, a *Karmayogi,* with predominantly religious and ethical bias. He always followed *dharma.* His approach was humanistic and eclectic. He synthesized the different strings of thought in a systematic view of life with well drawn code of conduct. Mahatma Gandhi's speeches and writings on 'Ethics' need to be understood in the light of above mentioned points.

The fundamental principles of Gandhian ethics can be formulated in terms of Truth, *Ahimsa* and *Satyagraha* or in terms of *swadeshi* and *Swaraj*. But different scholars, though unanimously agreeing on Truth and *Ahimsa*, have also selected some other principles of Mahatma Gandhi with varying emphasis in order to give a complete and comprehensive account of Gandhi's ethics, P.T. Raju in his article entitled "The Four Basic Principles of Gandhi's Philosophy" published in *Gandhi Marg* in 1957, holds the view that there are four basic postulates of Gandhian ethics : firstly, God is Truth; secondly, *Satyagraha;* thirdly, Finitude of man and his intellect, and fourthly, *Ahimsa.* Benoy Gopal Roy's *Gandhian Ethics* was published in 1950 by Navajivan. According to him the salient features of Gandhian Ethics or his principal vows are Truth, *Ahimsa,* Celibacy, Control of Palate, non-stealing and non-possession besides an added emphasis on the non-difference between Gandhi's concept of religion and morality. Navajivan published a small booklet entitled *Ethical Religion* in 1968 clearly describing ethics as morality and morality as a religion. Further there is no difference between social ideal and personal morality or religious morality or moral religion.

The moot question is whether we treat vows as ethical conduct or not. In 1929, C.F. Andrew, a close associate and friend of Gandhi, had given accounts of the vows of the Ashram as : Truth, *Ahimsa,* Celibacy, Control of Palate, Non-thieving, *Swadeshi,* Fearlessness, Removal of Untouchability, education through vernacular, and the vow of *Khaddar.* The complete account of these virtues and duties, in other words, the code of conduct offered by Mahatma Gandhi is found in From Yeravada Mandir and *Hindu Dharma,* the two books published by Navajivan. Gandhi's principles of good conduct known as *Ashram* vows, which are eleven in number, are basically ethics and ethical conduct, and are in conformity with his famous saying that "means and ends are convertible terms in my philosophy of life". For Gandhi there is no dichotomy between means and ends. Similarly, theory and practice, religion and morality, vows and ethical conduct are same. Gandhi's ethics and ethical conduct must be seen from *Anekanta* perspectives.

So when we work on "Gandhi on Ethics" and collect his writings and speeches, the above points need to be taken carefully. Gandhian ethics may be understood by identifying the fundamental ethical principles with some religious precepts. Gandhian ethics was more or less subjective in nature.

II

Gopinath Dhawan in his book, *The Political Philosophy of Mahatma Gandhi,* opines "His political philosophy and political techniques are only corollaries of his religious and moral principles".

Values and ethics determine how human beings behave. In traditional Indian thinking, the terms ethics, moral, *dharma* and even religion are commonly used interchangeably. Mahatma Gandhi's life is universally seen as representing amongst the highest standards of moral behaviour in all facets; individual, social, political, economic, moral and religious. Self-realization through selfless service of society, nation and humanity, was the key to his life and thought.

What should be the criteria of conditions of a moral action in Gandhian ethics? After an analysis the answer would be—an action is moral in Gandhian ethics of it is volitional, intentional, universal, practical, selfless, and free from fear and compulsion simultaneously. A moral action must be performed "consciously, deliberately with a determined will, regardless of gain or loss, of life or death, without turning to look back, ready to sacrifice themselves.[1]

The cultivation of calmness, wildness, and tranquillity of personality; fostering of good habits; observance of chastity, altruism and righteousness etc., are the elements of moral life in Gandhian ethics. Similarly, the moral law in Gandhian ethics is a pious; universal; eternal; immutable; independent of space and time; objective; self-imposed; dwells in the heart and deals with the inner being of our personalities. It is the highest; the best of all laws; supreme; divine, and unconditional imperative pregnant with its intrinsic value; and although mysterious unlocks the door to earthy necessities.

Anthony J. Parel in his latest book, *Gandhi's Philosophy and the Quest for Harmony*, 2006, rightly mentioned that a number of approaches to the study of Gandhi's thought are in vogue today—the Nationalist, the Marxist, the Orientalist, the Post-colonial, the Subaltern, to mention a few. Their common drawback is their inability to see that the theory of *purusharthas* is the key to his thought.[2] The theory of the *purusharthas* is a fundamental theory of Indian civilization. It is also the key to a deeper understanding of Gandhi's philosophy. His reinterpretation of this theory is one of his great contributions to modern Indian political thought. The traditional accounts of his contributions tend to list such ideas as *ahimsa, swaraj, satyagraha, swadeshi,* religion and

1. M.K. Gandhi, *Ethical Religion*, Ahmedabad, Navajivan, 1968, p. 19.
2. Anthony J. Parel, *Gandhi's Philosophy and the Quest for Harmony*, New Delhi, Cambridge University Press, 2006, p. viii.

sarvodaya.[1] To get the full picture we have to look for the intellectual framework within which they are set. The theory of the *purusharthas* proves to be that framework. To understand Gandhi adequately then, we have to understand his reinterpretation of this theory. The basic insight of the theory of the *purusharthas* is simple enough. A well-lived life requires the coordinated pursuit of all the four canonical goals of life; wealth and power (*artha*) ethics of duty based on experience (*dharma*), pleasure both sexual and aesthetic (*varna*), and spiritual freedom (*moksha*).[2]

Gandhi redefined *purushartha* as a spiritual ability that humans have to grasp what the worthwhile goals of life are, and, once grasped, to pursue them with determination and skill. "Our *purushartha* lies in striving to overcome whatever weakness we see in ourselves". Weakness that afflict Indians may arise from any number of sources—the colonial condition, caste oppression, or submission to fate (*vidhi*). *Purushartha* is the common antidote to all these weaknesses. Its recovery is the secret of India's innovation.[3]

Gandhi showed the way to harmonize the values of *artha* and *moksha*, secularism and spirituality, power and justice. *Purusharthas*, as interpreted by Gandhi, provide a set of values and ideals within which public discourse in India can (and should) be conducted. He presents a balanced view of life. Wealth, power, pleasure, aesthetic beauty, ethical integrity and freedom of the spirit, the *purusharthas*, are goals that all Indians seek. Gandhi explains how and why that seeking should be the basis of modern India's public philosophy.[4]

---

1. *Ibid.*, p. vii.
2. *Ibid.*
3 *Ibid.*, p. x.
4. *Ibid.*, p. xi.

The concept of *purushartha* has three related meanings. First, it means any human striving, secondly, it refers to human striving directed towards overcoming fate and *karma,* and thirdly, it refers to any one of the four canonically recognized aims of life, viz., *dharma* (ethics and religion), *artha* (wealth and power), *karma* (pleasure) and *moksha* (liberation from *samsara,* the cycle of birth, death and rebirth.[1]

Gandhi introduced several new things into the theory of the *purusharthas.* First, he removed the perceived gender bias from the concept. Second, he pointed out that the ability to pursue *purushartha* was unique to human beings, distinguishing them from all other living things. Third, he emphasized its role in overcoming fate and *karma.* Fourth, he gave the value of *artha* an unprecedented dignity and importance. And finally, he made the theory of the *purusharthas* the framework of his philosophy.[2]

The aim of Gandhi's practical philosophy was to create a new legacy in place of the old. He used the theory of the *purusharthas* to accomplish it. As a result it has become the framework of analysis of his basic ideas. Firstly, *purushartha* refers to the inner spiritual power that is present in all human beings. When rightly exercised it cannot only overcome all human weakness, even fate, but also enable humans to achieve transcendence. Secondly, they refer to the four goals pursued by individuals and cultures. The two meanings taken together constitute Gandhi's theory of the practical.

Gandhi used the concept of *dharma* in three senses : as duty, religion and ethics. The whole discourse of ethics and ethical conducts evolve around *purushartha.*

---

1. *Ibid.,* p. 5.
2. *Ibid.,* p. 14.

III

In 1907, Gandhi wrote the booklet entitled Ethical Religion as a summary (in Gujarati) of the book on *Ethical Religion* by William MacIntyre Salter, the founder of the Society for Ethical Culture, Chicago, and published in America in March 1889 and later in England in 1905. This booklet gives a peep into the philosophical premises of Gandhian ethics. The whole text is placed in part one and some excerpts from *Ethical Religion* are placed below :

- ... it is one's duty to obey the laws of ethics whether or not one professes a religion; and that even who would not obey them could do no good either to themselves or to others, in this world or the next. [*Ethical Religion*, p. 6].
- ... an ethical idea is useless so long as it is not followed by suitable action. There are many who memorize moral precepts and preach sermons, but they neither practice them nor do they mean to do so. There are some who believe that moral principles are not intended to be practiced in this world; they are meant for the other world— the world which lies beyond death. [*Ethical Religion*, p. 7].
- In the path of morality there is no such thing as reward for moral behaviour. If a man does some good deed, he does not do it to win applause, he does it because he must. For him doing good is but a higher kind of food, if one may compare food and goodness. And if someone should give him an opportunity to do a good deed, he would feel grateful just as a starving man would be grateful to the giver of food and bless him. [*Ethical Religion*, p. 8].

- ... there is no morality in my living a simple and unpretentious life if I have not the means to live otherwise. But plain, simple living would be moral if, though wealthy, I think of all the want and misery in the world about me—and feel that I ought to live a plain, simple life and not one of ease and luxury. [*Ethical Religion,* p. 13].
- ... moral strength is supreme. The ancient Greeks had greater intelligence than the Europeans of today, but when the former gave up morality, their intelligence became their enemy, and no trace of them remain today. Nations are sustained neither by wealth nor by armies, but by righteousness alone. It is the duty of man to bear this truth in mind and practice altruism; which is the highest form of morality. [*Ethical Religion,* p. 25].

Gandhi himself beautifully sums up, he alone is religious, he alone is happy and he alone is wealthy, who is sincere in himself, bears no malice, exploits no one and always acts with a pure mind. Such men alone can serve mankind.[1]

In 1909, while returning from London to South Africa by the ship, Gandhi wrote a small book containing 30,000 words in Gujarati in the form of a dialogue. This book is a masterpiece and contains profound ethical observations about *swaraj, swadeshi,* civilization, means and ends, duties and rights and provides, for the first time, a coherent rationale of non-violent resistance to injustice and evil. *Hind Swaraj* is a source book for evaluation of India and Indians. It is a manual of action for people.

From Yervada Mandir is written in 1930. In 1930 Gandhi was in the Yervada Central Prison. Gandhi wrote

1. M.K. Gandhi, *Ethical Religion,* Ahmedabad, Navajivan, 1968, p. 31.

weekly letters to the Satyagraha Ashram, containing a cursory examination of the principal Ashram observances. To Gandhi, *'ashrams'* were not places of withdrawal from the world but were training camps where inmates learnt how to devote themselves to active service of the society and the nation. This booklet is a gold-mine of Gandhi's views on the principles of ethics and ethical conducts.

Lastly, constructive programme : Its meaning and place was written in 1941. This booklet is a valuable guide on ethics for both the social workers engaged in public or voluntary service and the *satyagrahis,* as well as in the right approach to a welfare society or *sarvodaya.* Originally Gandhi selected eighteen areas for constructive work subsequently his followers add more as per demand of time and situation.

IV

Gandhi's ultimate source of ethics is from Indian scriptures. Gandhi memorized the *Gita,* which had become for him an "infallible guide of conduct" "a dictionary of daily reference".[1] His appreciation of *aparigraha* made him conceal the only insurance policy he ever took out in life, an act of rare faith. He resolved that thenceforth his savings would only be utilized for public work. In a letter to Lakshmidas, his elder brother, he declared : "I do not claim anything as mine. All that I have is being utilized for public purposes ... I have no desire for wordly enjoyments of any type whatever".[2] Another development was his growing conviction of the need for *brahamacharya* in a public worker. He had not then recognized its value for self-realization. But during the difficult marches that

1. *The Collected Works of Mahatma Gandhi,* New Delhi, Publication Division, Vol. 39, p. 11.
2. *CWMG* : 5 : 334-345.

had to be performed with the Stretcher-bearer Corps at the time of the Zulu Rebellion, he has recorded, "the idea flashed upon me that, if I want to devote myself to the service of the community in this manner, I must relinquish the desire for children and wealth, lead the life of a *vanaprastha,* of one retired from household affairs".[1] Being convinced that he "could not live both after the flesh and the spirit", Gandhi took in his 37th year, a vow of *brahmacharya* for life. Finally, it was the mass meeting of September 11, 1906 that he discovered the beauty and power of a pledge taken, with God as witness, to suffer all the penalties of non-submission to a bad law, and then the principle which later came to be called *satyagraha* took birth.

Service of the Harijans and of the poor was for Gandhiji part of his search for God. Speaking at a labourer's meeting he said : "There is only one joy for me and that is to get glimpse of God. This will be possible when I become one with the poor. I can be one with the whole world if I can merge myself in the poor people of a poor country".[2] "Man's ultimate aim", Gandhiji told Maurice Frydman, a Polish engineer "is the realization of God, and all his activities, social, political, religious, have to be guided by ultimate aim of the vision of God... the only way to find God is to see him in His creation and be one with it". "This", Gandhi added, "can only be done by service of all", which meant service of one's countrymen who were one's "nearest neighbours".[3] As he explained to a *Sadhu,* "we can but serve that part of God's creation which is nearest and best known to us.[4]

1. *CWMG* : 39 : 167.
2. *CWMG* : 63 : 406.
3. *CWMG* : 63 : 240.
4. *CWMG* : 63 : 233.

Moral purity was equally important. "However accomplished a man", Gandhiji wrote to A.V. Thakkar, "if he is immoral the splashes from the mud of his immorality are bound to stain public life".[1] When they had enough such "selfless, spiritually-minded" workers, then alone would the change of heart necessary for removal of untouchability come.[2]

No sooner had the Congress Ministries assumed office than Gandhi threw open the columns of *Harijan* for the "political education" of the new rulers and started a series of articles on their duties and responsibilities. In a personal letter to Jawaharlal Nehru he almost apologized for waning, and sought his permission for continuing, "to interfere with your handling of the whole situations", but he felt that it was his "duty to write".[3] Through these *Harijan* articles he advised the ministers to preserve "rigorous simplicity" in their style of living and also to introduce in the administration.[4] They had a vast opportunity now of achieving the Congress objectives if only they were "honest, selfless, industrious, vigilant and solicitous for the true welfare of the starving millions.[5] This programme of a moral and social revolution through democratic means required patient education of the public and Gandhiji set about the task through his articles in *Harijan*. Ministership, Gandhiji stressed, were not prizes but "avenues to service" and had "to be held lightly, not tightly".[6] Gandhi expected the Congress to rule "not through the police backed by the military but through its moral authority based upon the greatest goodwill of the

1. *CWMG* : 63 : 289.
2. *CWMG* : 63 : 181.
3. *CWMG* : 65 : 395.
4. *CWMG* : 65 : 407.
5. *CWMG* : 65 : 432.
6. *CWMG* : 66 : 16.

people "won through" the service of the people whom it seeks to represent in every one of its actions".[1] And he expected the same public spirit from the critics of the ministers. While he asserted that "it is not only a right, but a duty for any Congressmen to openly criticize acts of Congress officials", he also insisted that the "criticism has got to be courteous and well-informed"[2]. Healthy, well-informed, balanced criticism is the ozone of public life", Gandhi said.[3] Gandhi's advice to the ministers not to rule through the police did not mean, however, that they should tolerate violence. "Civil liberty is not criminal liberty", Gandhi stated emphatically. In the talks to the Khudai Khidmatgars the emphasis was on non-violence and service. "A small body of determined spirits, fired by an unquenchable faith in their mission can alter the course of history. It has happened before and it may again happen if the non-violence of Khudai Khidmatgars is unalloyed gold, not mere glittering tinsel".[4]

Pandit Jawaharlal Nehru had called Khadi "the livery of freedom" and Gandhi said : "To wear Khadi is to me to wear freedom... Freedom is never dear at any price. It is the breath of life. What would a man not pay for living"? Khadi alone provided "dignified labour to the millions who are otherwise idle for nearly four months in the year...if millions live in compulsory idleness, they must die spiritually, mentally and physically".[5] The constructive programme was an instrument of permanent value.

Gandhi was ever ready to conceal that "there may be a different way and a better way than mine of doing a thing".[6] He said : "There is always a saving clause about

---

1. *CWMG* : 66 : 62.
2. *CWMG* : 66 : 155-56.
3. *CWMG* : 66 : 292.
4. *CWMG* : 68 : 81.
5. *CWMG* : 68 : 174.
6. *CWMG* : 69 : 256.

all my advice. No one need to follow it unless it appeals to his head to heart. No one who has honestly the inner call need be deterred from obeying it because of my advice".[1] The best should not become an enemy of the good and non-violence of courage. The last thing he wanted was that our people not should be turned into cowards. He would far rather that people" died bravely dealing a blow and receiving a blow than died in abject terror".[2]

No ideal, Gandhi conceded, could be realized in full but he claimed that pleasure lies in making the effort, not in its fulfilment. Gandhi himself stated, "my aim is not to be consistent with my previous statement on a given question, but to be consistent with truth as it may present itself to me at given moment. The result has been that I have grown from truth to truth.[3]

"Freedom of speech and pen", Gandhi argued at A.I.C.C. meeting "is the foundation of *swaraj*. If the foundation stone is in danger, you have to exert the whole of your might in order to defend that single stone".[4] Though a *Karmayogi* par excellence, Gandhi knew the limitations of action. He thought of a person "whose intellect is clear and whose aspirations are pure", he wrote to Vinoba Bhave's brother, "have a power not to be found in his actions. Just as speech limits thought, so also action limits aspirations.[5] Gandhi's life-long interest in problems of physical and moral well-being led him to the conclusion. "Evil thoughts are also a sign of illness".[6] And he knew in his own experience the meaning of spiritual wholeness.

1. *CWMG* : 69 : 401.
2. *CWMG* : 69 : 313.
3. *CWMG* : 70 : 203.
4. *CWMG* : 73 : 21.
5. *CWMG* : 75 : 48-9.
6. *CWMG* : 78 : 395.

Even while he was thinking of a fast, he could feel "the joy of living". Answering a request for a message for the Negro people of America, Gandhi says : "my life is its own message".[1]

Gandhi wrote to an American friend, "The Kingdom of God is within you, is all-sufficient. Follow it out in action and you need nothing else".[2] His ideal polity was a means and a medium for the evaluation of means a moral and social being, a blending of man's perpetual aspiration for spiritual perfection with the modern ideals of justice and equality. Egoless service brought transparent purity and strength of mind. "A drop which has merged in the sea does not rot, but lends the sea its greatness... You can see clearly through a glass window. If you coat the pane with mercury, you will see none but yourself".[3] Integrity of conduct, the honest practice of what one professes, binds individual and society and raises political action to the level of spiritual *sadhana.* Self-reliance and single-minded performance of one's *swadharma* are the source as well as the result of happiness. Gandhi taught this one lesson to friends and followers who looked to him for guidance whether in private or public; "we should blame no one except ourselves. That is the only way to be happy in life and remain clean".[4] If you see only the fault in yourself and only the virtues in others, you will advance fast, be happy and never experience sorrow. We have no right to expect anything from anyone".[5] Meekness, however, is not weakness and non-violence is not cowardice. In fact, cowardice is "violence double distilled".[6] And if

1. *CWMG* : 80 : 209.
2. *CWMG* : 81 : 162.
3. *CWMG* : 85 : 464.
4. *CWMG* : 85 : 205.
5. *CWMG* : 85 : 300.
6. *CWMG* : 85 : 11.

oppression is than sin, submission to violence is no less sin.[1] Non-violence is the noblest virtue because it is the highest manliness.

Gandhi was firm in his faith that the lasting cure for all violence (whether inter-religious or international) was to be found in the moral transformation of human being rather than in any institutional arrangements. He hold further that the spiritual resources to bring about this necessary and possible change were already available in the great religions of the world and that India with its tradition of tolerance and pluralism provided the most congenial soil for the active pursuit of the spiritual value of universal brotherhood.

Gandhi's life-long mission was to educate people and teach them self-reliance for self-rule. If the people were ignorant they would be exploited. When the people realized their strength and the fact that the bottom sustained the top, it would be well within them.[2] Trusting the inarticulate wisdom Gandhi hoped to "educate" leaders by entrusting them with responsibility and letting them learn by listening and responding to the people.

The guiding principle of ethics was summed up beautifully in the talisman Gandhi gave to a co-worker. The politicians, policy maker, social worker and every citizen must remember this talisman.

> *"I will give you a Talisman. Whenever you are in doubt, or when the self becomes too much with you, apply the following test.*
>
> *Recall the face of the poorest and the weakest man whom you may have seen, and ask yourself, if the step you contemplate is going to be of any use to him? Will he gain anything by it? Will it restore him to a control over his*

1. *CWMG* : 85 : 73.
2. *CWMG* : 86 : 466.

> *own life and destiny? In other words, will it lead to swaraj for the hungry and spiritually starving millions? Then you will find your doubts and yourself melting away."*[1]

In a democracy, government should trust the people and educate them in and through the exercise of freedom. "Real democracy people learn not from books, not from the government who are in name and in reality their servants. Hard experience is the most efficient teacher in democracy.[2] Gandhi had unbounded faith in the inborn goodness of the common people and their capacity to learn. People should be educated in freedom so that they could "keep the ministers on their toes"[3]. A good government should ensure both freedom and welfare and thus promote the largest good of the people with the minimum of controls.[4]

On December 11 and 12, 1947 he called a meeting of various constructive work organizations and told them that "the social order of our dreams cannot come through the congress of today; that the task of the constructive workers was to "improve our national character", that with imagination and intellect these institutions could be forged into "instruments for the building up democracy", and that this aim could be achieved only if they kept away from the competition for political power.[5]

"... all rights to be deserved and preserved came from duty well done. Thus the very right to live accrues to us only when we do the duty of citizenship of the world. From this one fundamental statement, perhaps it is easy

1. *CWMG* : 89 : 125.
2. *CWMG* : 90 : 399.
3. *CWMG* : 90 : 391.
4. *CWMG* : 90 : 325.
5. *CWMG* : 90 : 215-23.

enough to define the duties of man and woman and corresponding duty to be first performed. Every other right can be shown to be usurpation... worth fighting for. I wonder if it is too late to revise the idea of defining the right of man apart from his duty.[1]

Gandhi wanted to make his associates responsible person in every field. Whether it is home or office or *ashram*, one has to observe perfect discipline. For Gandhi there is no dichotomy between private and public life. In money matter too, he insisted on a fool-proof system of keeping a detailed account. "Even if the money is one's own, one should keep a detailed account of every *kori* spent, for the fact is that nothing in this world is our own. It is our daily experience that everything belongs to God. We should, therefore, be very reasonable in the way we use things and spend our money. He who lives in this world keep for his own satisfaction an account of every pie spent by him".[2]

Mahatma Gandhi is universally accepted as an exemplary model of ethical and moral life with a rare combination between the personal and the public life, the individual and the social, the theory and the practice, thought and action, the eternal and the immediate. He was truly a *'karamyogi'* in *Gita*'s terminology. He considered life to be an integrated whole, to be lived as a series of "experiments with truth" thus growing in ethics and ethical conducts (moral status) each day. He took the existing religious and social precepts, fought to remove the 'excrescence', and worked incessantly, he died, through selfless service as the way to God and to self-realization. Towards the end Gandhi could truly say, "my life is my message". To Mahatma Gandhi, one's moral or ethical code must not follow from a self-righteous or self-

1. *CWMG* : 95 : 142.
2. *CWMG* : 97 : 23.

centred attitude but from a concern to be humble, right, just and true towards others. His over 78 years of life included over 54 years of public life which he lived as an open book and never deviated from *dharma,* righteousness is the King of Kings—*Dharmaman Kshatrasaya Kshatram.* Gandhian doctrine of the supreme importance of the purity of means and of moral values are the need of the hour when even *satyam* (truth) have become *asatyam* (untruth). In fact, Gandhi was emphasizing the historical urgency of resuming his original task, the task he had formulated in *Hind Swaraj* in 1909. Through *Hind Swaraj* Gandhi wanted to establish self-esteem of individual and moral regeneration of India. In other words, Gandhi through *Hind Swaraj* wanted to transform (a) India as a nation and polity, and (b) Indians !

While speaking on the objective resolution in the Constituent Assembly, Nehru referred to Gandhiji as the "architect of this Assembly and all that has gone before it and probably of much that will follow". These last few words expressed Nehru's belief that Gandhian principles will continue to govern the affairs of the Indian Republic, so do the words from his statement following Gandhiji's assassination :

The light has gone out, I said and yet I was wrong ... the light that has illumined this country for these many years will illumine this country for many more years and a thousand years later that light will still be seen in this country and the world will see it and it will give solace to innumerable hearts. For that light represented the living truth... the eternal truths, reminding us of the right path, drawing us from error, taking this ancient country to freedom.

To understand Gandhiji amidst his conflicting statements, one has perhaps to go into the meaning of meaning. "To know their deeper significance, going by the literal meaning of words would be futile and burdensome".[1] Gandhiji is also confronted with upheavals within and without. So at times we have to go into the meaning of meaning to understand what he really means.

Gandhi on ethics may be summed up under the title "Seven Social Sins" which Gandhi wrote in *Young India* of 22.10.1925 :

Politics without principles
Wealth without work
Pleasure without conscience
Knowledge without character
Commerce without morality
Science without humanity
Worship without sacrifice.

1. *CWMG* : 93 : 153.

PART TWO

ETHICAL RELIGION BY M.K. GANDHI

2

Introduction

Hypocrisy has nowadays increased in the world. Whatever a man's religion, he thinks only of its outward form and fails in his real duty. In our crazy pursuit of wealth, we seldom think of the harm we cause, or are likely to cause, to others. Women in Europe do not hesitate in the least to wear soft [kid] gloves even though these are made by killing young and tender animals. It is known the world over how Mr. Rockefeller, said to be the richest man in the world, violated many rules of morality in amassing his fortune. It is because such conditions prevail around them that many people in Europe and America have turned against religion. They argue that, if any religion worth the name existed in the world, the inordinate wickedness that is rampant all round would not be there. This is a mistaken view. As it is common for a workman to quarrel with his tools and not try to look for his own faults, so, instead of thinking of the wickedness in themselves, men brand religion itself as humbug and go on acting and living as they please.

Observing this trend and fearing that, if all religions are destroyed, a great calamity may befall the world and people may forsake the moral path altogether, many Americans and Europeans have come forward to try, in a variety of ways, to bring the people back to that path.

A Society[1] has been founded which has shown, after an investigation of all religions, that not only do all of them teach morality but they are based for the most part on ethical principles; that it is one's duty to obey the laws of ethics whether or not one professes a religion; and that men who would not obey them could do no good either to themselves or to others, in this world or the next. The object of these societies is to influence those who have led to look down upon all religions because of the prevailing hypocrisy. They find out the fundamentals of all religions, discuss and write about the ethical principles common to them and live up to them. This creed they call Ethical Religion. It is not among the aims of these societies to criticize any religion. Men professing all religions can, and do, join these societies. The advantage of such a society is that members adhere to their own faith more strictly and pay greater attention to its moral teaching. They firmly believe that man ought to abide by the laws of morality and that if he does not, it means an end to all order in the world and ultimate destruction.

Mr. Salter, a learned American, has published a book on the subject, which is excellent. Though it does not deal with any religion as such, it contains teachings of universal application. We shall publish the substance of these teachings every week. All that needs to be said about the author is that he practises whatever he advises others to do. We would only appeal to the reader to try to live up to those moral precepts that appeal to him. Then only may we regard our efforts as having been fruitful.

1. The Society for Ethical Culture, Chicago.

3

Beginning

It is the moral nature of man by which he rises to good and noble thoughts. The different sciences show us the world as it is. Ethics tells us what it ought to be. It enables man to know how he should act. Man has two windows to his mind : through one he can see his own self as it is; through the other, he can see what it ought to be. It is our task to analyse and explore the body, the brain and the mind of man separately; but if we stop here, we derive no benefit despite our scientific knowledge. It is necessary to know about the evil effects of injustice, wickedness, vanity and the like, and the disaster they spell where the three are found together. And mere knowledge is not enough, it should be followed by appropriate action. An ethical idea is like an architect's plan. The plan shows how the building should be constructed; but it becomes useless if the building is not raised accordingly. Similarly, an ethical idea is useless so long as it is not followed by suitable action. There are many who memorize moral precepts and preach sermons, but they neither practise them nor do they mean to do so. There are some who believe that moral principles are not intended to be practised in this world; they are meant for the other world—the world which lies beyond death. A great thinker has said, "If you wish to attain perfection, you must begin from this very day to live according to the laws of morality at any cost." We need not be scared away by such thoughts; on the contrary we should be glad to live up to them, considering our responsibility in the matter. "Certainly, cousin," said the gallant Earl of Pembroke, on coming up to the Earl of Derby before Aubercoche and finding the battle already won, "you have neither been courteous nor behaved honourably to fight my enemies without waiting for me, seeing that you had sent for me". Only when there is such readiness to accept moral responsibility will men tread the path of virtue.

God is omnipotent, He is perfect. There are no limits to His mercy, to His goodness and to His justice. If this is so, how can we, His bond slaves, stray at all from the moral path? It is no fault of the ethical principles if one following them should fail. However, those committing a breach of morality have only themselves to blame.

In the path of morality there is no such thing as reward for moral behaviour. If a man does some good deed, he does not do it to win applause; he does it because he must. For him doing good is but a higher kind of food, if one may compare food and goodness. And if someone should give him an opportunity to do a good deed, he would feel grateful just as a starving man would be grateful to the giver of food and bless him.

This ethical religion, of which we have spoken, does not mean the cultivation of gentlemanliness. It does mean that we should become a little more diligent, a little better educated, a little cleaner and neater, etc. All this is no doubt included in it, but it touches only the fringe of ethical religion. Many more things have to be done by man if he would walk along this path; and he has to do them as a matter of duty, knowing them to be a part of his nature, not for gaining any worldly benefit.

4

Ideal Morality

The current views of morality are not of a very high order. Some believe that morality is not something quite essential. Others think that there is no relation between religion and morality. But an examination of the world's religions shows that without morality, religion cannot subsist. True morality covers religion for the most part. Anyone who observes the laws of morality for their own sake and not for any selfish end can be regarded as religious. There are men in Russia who dedicate their lives to the good of their country. Such men are truly moral. A man like Jeremy Bentham, who discovered many good principles for English legislation, tried very hard to spread education among the English and took a prominent part in improving the condition of prisoners, may be regarded as truly moral.

Besides, it is a rule of ideal morality that it is not enough to follow the trodden path. We ought to follow the path which we know to be true, whether it is familiar or unfamiliar to us. In other words, when we know a particular path to be the right one, we should set out on it without fear. We can progress only if we observe the laws of morality in this way. That is why true morality, true civilization and true progress are always to be found together.

If we examine our desires, we shall see that we do not wish for what we have already. We always value more that which we do not have. But desires are of two kinds : one is the pursuit of mere self-interest. To attempt to fulfil this kind of desire is immoral. The other impels us constantly to improve ourselves and to do good to others.We should never become overweening with any amount of good that we may do. It is not for us to evaluate it, but rather should we have perpetual longing to become better and do more good. True morality consists in our effort to realize such longing.

If we have no home or family of our own, that is nothing to be ashamed of. But if we have a home and abuse it, or own a business and practise fraud, we stray from the path of morality. Morality consists in doing what we ought to do. We can prove the need of morality through a few illustrations. Destruction has been the lot of peoples or families in which the seeds of immorality, such as disunity and untruth, were found. To take an example from trade and business, we do not come across a single person who will say that truth should not be followed. The effect of justice and goodness is not felt from outside; these qualities are inhere in us. Four hundred years ago, much injustice and untruth prevailed in Europe, so that people could not rest in peace even for a moment. The cause of this state of affairs was that people had no morality. If we take out the essence of all moral laws, we shall find that the attempt to do good to mankind is the highest morality. If we open the treasure house of morality with this key, we shall find in it all the other principles.

At the end of each of these articles, we print select poems bearing on morality from Gujarati or Urdu poets in the hope that all our readers will benefit from them and will also commit them to memory. We begin with an extract[1] from Mr. Malbari's[2] book, *Adam Ane Teni Duniya.*

1. Not reproduced here.
2 B.M. Malbari, Gujarati poet and social reformer. The title of the book is *Man and His World.*

5

What is Moral Action?

When can it be said that a particular action is moral? In asking this question, the intention is not to contrast moral with immoral actions, but to consider many of our everyday actions against which nothing can be said from the conventional standpoint and which some regard as moral. Most of our actions are probably non-moral; they do not necessarily involve morality. For the most part we act according to the prevailing conventions. Such conventional behaviour is often necessary. If no such rules are observed, anarchy would be the result, and society—social intercourse—would come to an end. Still the mere observance of custom and usage cannot properly be called morality.

A moral act must be our own act : it must spring from our own will. If we act mechanically, there is no moral content in our act. Such action would be moral, if we think it proper to act like a machine and do so. For in doing so, we use our discrimination. We should bear in mind the distinction between acting mechanically and acting intentionally. It may be moral of a king to pardon a culprit. But the messenger bearing the order of pardon plays only a mechanical part in the king's moral act. But if the messenger were to bear the king's order, considering it to be his duty, his action would be a moral one. How can a man understand morality who does not use his own intelligence and power of thought, but lets himself be swept along like a log of wood by a current? Sometimes a man defies convention and acts on his own with a view to [doing] absolute good. Such a great hero was Wendell Phillips[1]. Addressing an assembly of people, he once said, "Till you learn to form your own opinions and express them, I do not care much what you think of me." Thus when we all care only for what our conscience says, then alone can we be regarded to have stepped on to the moral road. We shall not reach this stage, as long as we do not believe—and experience the belief—that God within us, the God of all, is the ever present witness to all our acts.

It is not enough that an act done by us is in itself good; it should have been done with the intention to do good. That is to say, whether an act is moral or otherwise depends upon the intention of the doer. Two men may have done exactly the same thing; but the act of one may be moral, and that of the other the contrary. Take, for instance, a man who out of great pity feeds the poor and another who does the same, but with the motive of winning prestige or with some such selfish end. Though the action is the same, the act of the one is moral and that of the other non-moral. The reader here ought to remember the distinction between the two words, non-moral and immoral. It may be that we do not always see good results flowing from a moral act. While thinking of morality, all that we need to see is that the act is good and is done with a good intention. The result of an action is not within our control. God alone is the giver of fruit. Historians have called Emperor Alexander "great". Wherever he went [in the course of his conquests,] he took the Greek language and Greek culture, arts and manners, and today we enjoy the benefits of Greek civilization. But

1. (1811-84); American orator, social reformer and abolitionist.

the intention of Alexander behind all this was only conquest and renown. Who can, therefore, say that his actions were moral? It was all right that he was termed "great", but moral he cannot be called.

These reflections prove that it is not enough for a moral act to have been done with a good intention, but it should have been done without compulsion. There is no morality whatever in my act, if I rise early out of the fear that, if I am late for my office, I may lose my situation. Similarly there is no morality in my living a simple and unpretentious life if I have not the means to live otherwise. But plain, simple living would be moral if, though wealthy, I think of all the want and misery in the world about me—and feel that I ought to live a plain, simple life and not one of ease and luxury. Like wise it is only selfish, and not moral, of an employer to sympathize with his employees or to pay them higher wages lest they leave him. It would be moral if the employer wished well of them and treated them kindly realizing how he owed his prosperity to them. This means that for an act to be moral it has to be free from fear and compulsion. When the peasants rose in revolt and with bloodshot eyes went to King Richard II of England demanding their rights, he granted them the rights under his own seal and signature. But when the danger was over, he forced them to surrender the letters. It would be a mistake for anyone to say that King Richard's first act was moral and the second immoral. For his first act was done only out of fear and had not an iota of morality about it.

Just as a moral action should be free from fear or compulsion so should there be no self-interest behind it. This is not to say that actions prompted by self-interest are all worthless, but only that to call them moral would detract from the [dignity of the] moral idea. That honesty cannot long endure which is practised in the belief that it is the best policy. As Shakespeare says, love born out of the profit motive is no love.[1]

Just as an action prompted by the motive of material gain here on earth is non-moral, so also another done for considerations of comfort and personal happiness in another world is non-moral. That action is moral which is done only for the sake of doing good. A great Christian, St. Francis Xavier, passionately prayed that his mind might always remain pure.[2] For him devotion to God was not for enjoying a higher seat after death. He prayed because it was man's duty to pray. The great Saint Theresa wished to have a torch in her right hand and a vessel of water in her left, so that with the one she might burn the glories of heaven and with the other extinguish the fires of hell, and men might learn to serve God from love alone— without fear of hell and without temptation of heavenly bliss. To preserve morality thus demands a brave man prepared to face even death. It is cowardice to be true to friends and to break faith with enemies. Those who do good out of fear and haltingly have no moral virtue. Henry Clay, known for his kindliness, sacrificed his convictions to his ambition. Daniel Webster[3], for all his great intellect and

---

1. "Love is not love,
   When it is mingled with respects that stand
   Aloof from the entire point."
2. *"Then why, O blessed Jesus Christ,*
   Shall I not love thee well?
   Not for the sake of winning heaven,
   Or of escaping hell;
   Not with the hope of gaining aught,
   Not seeking a reward—
   But as thyself hast loved me,
   O everlasting Lord !"
3. (1782-1852); American statesman and lawyer; his "biographers insist that he was never personally dishonest" —*Encyclopaedia Britannica*

his sense of the heroic and the sublime, once sold his intellectual integrity for a price. By a single mean act he wiped out all his good deeds. This shows how difficult it is to judge the morality of a man's action because we cannot penetrate the depths of his mind. We have also the answer to the question raised at the outset in this chapter : what is a moral action? Incidentally, we also saw which kind of men could live up to that morality.[1]

1. Here follows a poem from *Kavyadohan,* an anthology of Gujarati verse, but it is not reproduced in this book.

6

Is there a Higher Law ?

We constantly pronounce judgements upon the value of actions. Some actions satisfy us and others do not. Whether a certain act is good or bad does not depend upon whether it is beneficial or harmful to us. In judging it, we adopt quite a different standard. We have in our minds certain ideas and on the basis of those we judge the acts of others. Whether any wrong done by one to another affects us or not, we do feel it to be wrong. Sometimes we have a trace of sympathy for the wrong doer; but despite that sympathy, we feel no hesitation at all in pronouncing his act to be wrong. It may be that at times our judgement is found to be mistaken. We cannot always fathom a man's motives, and may thus judge him wrongly. Nevertheless, we find no difficulty in judging an act in so far as the intention is known. Even if our personal interests are sometimes served by wrong actions, we do feel inwardly that they are wrong.

Thus it is established that the rightness or wrongness of an act does not depend upon a man's self-interest. Nor does it depend upon his wishes. There is a difference between morality and sympathy. Out of sympathy for the child we wish to give it a certain thing, but if the thing is harmful to the child, we hold it immoral to give it. It is doubtless good to show sympathy but, unrestricted by moral considerations, it turns into poison.

We see also that moral laws are immutable. Opinions change, but not morality. When our eyes are open, we see the sun; when they are closed, it is not seen. The change here has been in our sense of sight, not in the fact of the sun's existence. The same holds true of moral laws. It is probable that in a state of ignorance we do not know what is moral; but once the eye of knowledge is opened, there is no difficulty in knowing it. Men rarely care to see single-mindedly the right or wrong of things; often prompted by personal considerations, they mistakenly describe the immoral as moral. The time is yet to come when men, freeing themselves from self-regarding considerations, will concentrate their attention on the ideas of morality alone. Moral culture is still in its mere infancy; it is as science was before the birth of a Bacon or a Darwin. Men were eager to know what the truth was. Instead of inquiring into morality, they have been hitherto engaged in discovering laws of nature the laws of the earth's motion, etc. Where do we find the disinterested student of morality, patient and painstaking, who, setting aside his earlier superstitious notions, devotes his life to seeking only the ideal good? When men become as eager to explore the world of moral ideas as they are now to explore the realms of nature, we shall be able to bring together the various conceptions of morality. It is unlikely that, on ideas of morality, there will be the same divergence of opinion as exists among men on matters of science. However, we may not for a time arrive at unanimity of opinion regarding moral laws. This does not, however, mean that it is impossible to distinguish between right and wrong.

We thus see that, independent of and apart from men's wishes and opinions, there is something like a moral standard which we may call moral law. If there are laws of the state, why may not there be a moral law too? It does not matter if that law is not committed to writing by man, and indeed it need not be. If we grant or hold that the moral law exists, it is incumbent on us to obey it, just as we ought to obey the law of the state. A moral law is distinct from and better than the laws of the state or those of business. One may ask, "How does it matter if I do not obey the laws of business and remain poor? Or if I disobey the laws of the state and incur the ruler's displeasure?" But it will never do—either for me or anyone else—to say, "What does it matter whether I tell a lie or tell the truth?"

There is thus a great difference between moral laws and temporal laws. For morality dwells in our hearts. Even a man practising immorality would admit that he has been immoral. A wrong can never become right. Even where a people is vile, though men may not observe the moral law, they would make a pretence of doing so; they thus are obliged to admit that moral laws ought to be observed. Such is the greatness of morality. It cares not for custom nor for public opinion. To a moral man, public opinion or custom is binding only so long as it is in harmony with the moral law.

Where does this moral law come from? This law is not laid down by the state, for different laws are found in different states. Many men were opposed to the morality which Socrates observed in his day. Even so the world admits that the morality he observed has remained, and shall remain, morality for ever. Robert Browning says, 'If ever Satan proclaimed the law of hatred and untruth in the world, even then justice, goodness and truth will continue to be divine."[1] One may conclude from this that the moral law is supreme and divine.

1. ...justice, good, and truth were still
Divine, if, by some demon's will,
Hatred and wrong had been proclaimed
Law through the worlds, and right misnamed.
Christmas Eve, XVII

Such a law no people or individual can violate to the end of time. As has been said, even as the dangerous storm ultimately passes, immoral men must meet their destruction.[1]

No sooner did the cup of sin in Assyria and Babylon become full than it broke. When Rome trod the path of immorality, none of her great men could save her. The ancient Greeks were an accomplished people, still all their art and philosophy could not continue in their immorality for long. The French Revolution was but an insurrection against immorality. The same was the case with America. The good Wendell Phillips used to say that immorality even if enthroned will not endure. This mysterious moral law brings prosperity to the man who observes it : it sustains the family that obeys it, and the community which lives by it ever flourishes. Freedom, peace and happiness are the lot of the nation that lets itself be ruled by this highest law.[2]

---

1. As the whirlwind passeth, so is the wicked no more; but the righteous is an everlasting foundation.

   Proverbs, X.25.

2. Here follows a poem from *Kavyadohan.*

7

Morality as a Religion

The subject of this chapter may strike one as strange. The common idea is that morality and religion are distinct things; still this chapter seeks to consider morality as a religion. Some readers may think the writer guilty of confusion. That reproach may come from two sides— from those who regard religion as more than morality, and from others who think that, where there is morality, there is no need for religion. Yet the author's intention is to show their close relationship. The societies spreading ethical religion or religious ethics believe in religion through morality.

The common idea, it may be admitted, is that there may be morality without religion and religion without morality. One comes across many men of immoral conduct who claim to be religious in spite of the sinful acts they commit. On the other hand, there are moral men like the late Mr. Bradlaugh, who are proud to call themselves atheists and would run away from the name of religion. Those who hold either of these views are mistaken. Those who hold the first view are not only mistaken, but also dangerous as they practise immorality under the guise of religion. In this chapter, therefore, we shall show that, considered intellectually and scientifically, religion and morality are united and should be so united.

Morality was in the beginning simply the customary conduct of a community, settled ways of acting that men living together naturally fell into. By a natural process the good customs tended to survive and the bad ones to die out, since, if the bad ones did not die out, they would weaken the community and lead to its extinction. Even today we see this process at work. It is neither morality nor religion if people observe good customs more or less unthinkingly. However, most of what passes for morality in the world today consists, as pointed out above, of good customs.

Moreover, men often have a merely superficial idea of religion. Sometimes men believe in religion only as a means to ward off dangers that threaten them. It would be a mistake to dignify actions as religious where they are performed out of a love that springs from fear.

But at long last a time does come when men begin to tread the path of morality consciously, deliberately with a determined will, regardless of gain or loss, of life or death, without turning to look back, ready to sacrifice themselves. Then can they be said to have been permeated with true morality.

How can such morality subsist except with the support of religion? One tells oneself, "If by doing a little harm to another, I can secure my personal interest, why should I not do that little harm?" The profit derived from doing harm is no profit, but a positive loss [to the doer]. How shall this unpalatable dose go down one's throat? Ostensibly in Germany's interest, Bismarck perpetrated dreadful deeds. Where then was his education? Where did those maxims of morality disappear which, at other times, he used to mouth before school children? Obviously, a reply to all these questions can be given. The reason why he could not keep up his morality in the face of these difficulties was that his morality was not grounded in religion. So long as the seed of morality is not watered by religion, it cannot sprout. Without water it withers and ultimately perishes. Thus it will be seen that true or ideal morality ought to include true religion. To put the same thought differently, morality cannot be observed without religion. That is to say, morality should be observed as a religion.

Furthermore, it is seen that the rules of morality, laid down in the world's great religions, are largely the same. The founders of the religions have also explained that morality is the basis of religion. If a foundation is removed, the superstructure falls to the ground; similarly if morality is destroyed, religion which is built on it comes crashing down.

The author adds that there is nothing wrong in calling morality a religion. Dr. Coit in his prayer says, "I shall have no other God except righteousness." On reflection, we shall realize that God will not help us and answer our impassioned prayer for help, if we utter His name, while having a dagger concealed under our arm. Let us take two men, one who believes in the existence of God, yet breaks all His Commandments; and another who, though not acknowledging God by name, worships Him through his deeds and obeys His laws, recognizing in the divine laws, their Maker. Which of the two men shall we call a man of religion and morality? Without a moment's thought, one would emphatically reply that the second man alone is to be considered religious and moral.[1]

1. Here follows a poem by Behramji Malbari which has not been translated.

8

Religious Morality or Moral Religion

DARWIN'S VIEWS ON ETHICS

[Before summarizing this chapter, it is necessary to give an account first of Darwin himself. Darwin was a great Englishman of the last century who made great scientific discoveries. His memory and his power of observation were amazing. He has written some books which deserve to be read and pondered. With a mass of evidence and arguments, he has shown how man came into being; how he has evolved from a particular kind of monkey. After a large number of experiments and much sifting of evidence, he realized that there was not much difference between the anatomy of man and that of the ape. Whether this conclusion is correct or not has not much to do with ethics. Besides this, Darwin has also shown how ideas of morality affect mankind. And as many scholars have faith in Darwin's writings, our author has dealt with his views in Chapter VI.]

It is noble voluntarily to do what is good and right. The true sign of man's nobility is the fact that, instead of being driven about like a cloud before the wind, he stands firm and can do, and in fact does, what he deems proper.

Nevertheless, we ought to know the direction in which our environment disposes our instincts. We know that we are not in every way masters of our own life; there are conditions outside of us to which we have to adjust ourselves. For instance, in a country where Himalayan cold prevails, we have to put on adequate clothing, whether we like it or not, in order to keep the body warm. That is, we have to act with prudence.

The question now arises : does the influence of environment lead us to be moral? Or can it be that the forces that surround us are indifferent to morality?

At this point it becomes necessary to consider Darwin's views. Though Darwin did not write as a moral philosopher, he has shown how close the connection is between morality and environment. Those who think that morality is unimportant and that physical strength and mental capacity are the only things that matter should read Darwin. According to him, there is an instinct of self-preservation in men as in other creatures. He also says that those who survive the struggle for existence may be regarded as successful, that is, those who are unfit tend to extinction, but that the issue of the struggle does not depend on mere physical force.

Comparing man with the bear or the buffalo, we find that, in physical strength, the bear and the buffalo are superior to him; in a tussle he will surely be worsted. Nonetheless he is their superior by virtue of his intelligence. Similarly we can compare different races of men. In war it is not the side with the largest numbers or with the hardiest soldiers that wins, but the side with the ablest generals and the best strategy, though its soldiers may be fewer or less hardy. In these examples we see the superiority of intelligence.

But Darwin shows further that moral strength is even superior to physical and intellectual strength; and we can see in various ways that a man who has moral qualities lasts longer than one who is devoid of them. Some hold that Darwin taught that strength is enough; that is, those who are physically strong ultimately survive. Superficial thinkers may believe that morality is of no use. But this is not Darwin's view at all. We find from the evidence of the early history of man that races without morality have completely disappeared. The people of Sodom and Gomorrah were extremely immoral and they are now, therefore, completely extinct. We can see even today how races without morality are steadily declining.

Let us now take some simple illustrations and see how at least common morality is necessary for sustaining the human race. A peaceful disposition is one element of morality. At first sight it may appear that people with a violent disposition rise in life; but a little reflection will show that, when the sword of violence falls, it may be on one's own neck. Freedom from bad habits forms another element of morality. Statistics have proved that, at the age of thirty, intemperate persons in England are not likely to live beyond another thirteen or fourteen years, while the teetotaler's expectation of life is seventy years. Yet another element of morality is chastity. Darwin has shown that profligate persons die early. They have no children, or if they have any, they are weak. The profligate become feeble of mind, and in course of time look like idiots.

If we consider the morals of various communities, we find the same state of affairs. Among the Andaman islanders the husband looks after his wife only until their child is weaned and begins to move about, and he then abandons her. That is, they do not have the quality of altruism, and utter selfishness prevails. The result is that the race is gradually dying out. Darwin shows that the altruistic instinct is present, to some extent, even in animals : timid birds display strength in defending their young. This shows that, if there had been no selflessness among animals, we should have in the world scarcely any life other than grass and poisonous flora. The main distinction between man and other animals is that man is more selfless than the animals. He has sacrificed his life for others in proportion to his strength, that is, for his offspring, for his family, his community and his country.

Darwin clearly shows that moral strength is supreme. The ancient Greeks had greater intelligence than the Europeans of today, but when the former gave up morality, their intelligence became their enemy, and no trace of them remains today. Nations are sustained neither by wealth nor by armies, but by righteousness alone. It is the duty of man to bear this truth in mind and practise altruism, which is the highest form of morality.

9

Social Ideal

It is sometimes said that all morality involves social relations. This is well said; for instance, if the judge has a proper sense of justice, men who go to court obtain satisfaction. Similarly love, kindness, generosity and other qualities can be manifested only in relation to others. The force of loyalty can be demonstrated only in our relations with one another. Of patriotism, nothing need be said. Truly speaking, there is no aspect of morality the benefit of which accrues to the practitioner alone. Sometimes it is said that truthfulness and other virtues have nothing to do with the other person and are entirely personal. But we must admit that by telling the truth we prevent harm to another, just as by telling a lie and deceiving a person we do him an injury.

In the same way, when a man disapproves of certain laws or customs and withdraws from society, even then his acts affect society. Such a man lives in a world of ideals. He does not worry that the world of his ideals is not yet born. For him the mere thought that the prevailing standard is not good enough is sufficient to impel him to resist it. He will constantly try to change other people's way of life to his own. This is how prophets have caused the world's wheels to change their course.

So long as man remains selfish and does not care for the happiness of others, he is no better than an animal and perhaps worse. His superiority to the animal is seen only when we find him caring for his family. He is still more human, that is, much higher than the animal, when he extends his concept of the family to include his country or community as well. He climbs still higher in the scale when he comes to regard the human race as his family. A man is an animal or imperfect [as a human being] to the extent that he falls behind in his service to humanity. If I feel my wife's injury or that of my community, yet have no sympathy for anyone outside the circle, it is clear that I do not have any feeling for humanity as such; but I have, simply out of selfishness or a sense of discrimination, a certain feeling for my wife, my children or the community which I hold as my own.

That is to say, we have neither practised nor known ethical religion so long as we do not feel sympathy for every human being. Now we know that the higher morality must be comprehensive; it must embrace all men. Considering our relation to mankind, every man has a claim over us, as it is our duty always to serve him. We should act on the assumption that we have no claim on others. He is merely ignorant who would here argue that the man acting in this manner will be trampled in the world's scramble. For it is a universal experience that God always saves the man who whole-heartedly devotes himself to the service of others.

According to this moral standard all men are equal. This is not to be interpreted to mean equality of position and function for all. It only means that, if I hold a high place, I also have the ability to shoulder its duties and responsibilities. I should not, therefore, lose my head and believe that men with smaller responsibilities are my inferiors. Equality depends on the state of our mind, and until our mind reaches that state, we shall remain backward.

According to this moral standard no nation can rule another for selfish ends. It is immoral of the American people to reduce the aborigines to an inferior status and run the government. A civilized race coming into contact with a savage one owes it to the latter to raise it to its own level. The same standard rules that the king is the servant and not the master of his people and that the officers are not there to enjoy power but to make the people happy. If the people in a democratic state are selfish, that state comes to no good.

Moreover, according to this law, the stronger members of a state or community have to protect, not oppress, the weaker ones. Under such a government there can be no starvation; nor can there be excessive accumulation of riches; for we can never be happy while we see our neighbours languishing in misery. The man following this high moral standard will never amass wealth. He who would be moral need not bc scared away by the thought that few follow this ideal morality; for he is master of his morality, not of its results. He will be considered guilty if he does not practise morality; but nobody will find fault with him if his immoral behaviour has no consequences for society.

10

Personal Morality

'I am responsible for this,' or 'This is my duty' : this is a moving and wonderful thought. A mysterious, resounding voice seems to say, 'To thee, individually, O man, is given this task. Whether defeat or victory, both belong to thee. Thou art what no one else in the world is, for nowhere has nature created two similar objects. Thou hast a duty which no one else in the world can do, and if thou dost not do it that loss will stand debited to thee in the world's balance-sheet.'

'What is that duty I owe to myself?' Someone may quote the verse :

> Call not man God, for man is not God,
> Yet man is not distinct from God's glory,

and answer, 'My duty is to rest secure in the belief that I am a ray of God's light.' Another may answer that the duty is to have sympathy and fraternal regard for others. A third may answer that it is to revere parents, care for one's wife and children, and acquit oneself well with brother, sister or friend. Alongside of all these virtues, it is also a part of my duty to respect myself even as I respect others. As long as I do not understand myself, how shall I understand others? And how shall I respect one whom I do not know? Many hold the view that the obligation of proper conduct arises [only] in relation to others and that, in the absence of contact with others, one may do just as one pleases. He who holds this view does not know what he says. In this world none can, with impunity, act as he pleases.

Let us now see what our duty is to ourselves. Let us take, first, our private habits which are unknown to all but ourselves. We are responsible for them since they affect our character; but this is not all. We are responsible for them also because they affect others. Every person ought to control his own impulses, and keep his soul as well as body clean. 'Tell me,' says a great man, 'what a man's private habits are and I shall tell you what he is or will be'. We should, therefore, control all our appetites, so that we do not drink or eat to excess. Else we shall lose our strength and our good name. Worldly success never comes to him who does not abstain from sensual pleasures and does not thus save his body, mind, intellect and soul.

Arguing along these lines and keeping one's instincts pure, one should further consider how to put them to use. One ought to have a fixed aim in life. If we do not discover our life's purpose, and keep steadily to the course, we shall be swept along like a rudderless ship on the high seas; we shall falter on the [moral] path. Man's highest duty in life is to serve mankind and take his share in bettering its condition. This is true worship—true prayer. He is a godly man who does God's work. Hypocrites and cheats going about invoking God's name are legion. Because a parrot utters the name of God, no one would call it godly. Contribution to an ideal order of human life is something everyone can aim at. With this aim in view the mother may legitimately rear her child, the lawyer may pursue his profession, the merchant may carry on his business or trade and the working man may labour. A person with that fixed aim would never deviate from the path of morality, for if he did, he could not fulfil his aim of uplifting mankind.

Let us consider the matter in some detail. We ought constantly to examine whether our way of life tends to improve human life or to worsen it. Thus the merchant should ask himself whether, in transacting a business, he is cheating himself or another. The lawyer and the physician, acting according to this standard, will give more thought to their client or patient than to their fees. The mother in rearing her child would proceed very cautiously lest she should spoil the child out of misguided love or some selfish interest. The worker too would be guided by these considerations and do his duty. The result of all this would be that, if the worker fulfils his function in conformity with the moral ideal, he would be deemed better and higher than the wealthy merchant, physician or lawyer who lives without any discipline. The worker would be the true coin and those selfish men, even though more intelligent or wealthy, would be counterfeit. This further shows that any man, whatever his place in life, has the power to fulfil this aim. A man's value depends upon his way of life, not his status. One's way of life is not to be judged by one's visible outward actions, but by one's inner leanings. For instance, if of two men, one gives a dollar to a poor person to rid himself of his presence and the other half a dollar but with love and out of compassion for the man, obviously, the one who gave half a dollar is truly moral, while the other who gave a dollar, the sinner.

To sum up, he alone is religious, he alone is happy and he alone is wealthy, who is sincere in himself, bears no malice, exploits no one and always acts with a pure mind. Such men alone can serve mankind. How can a damp matchstick kindle a log of wood? How can a man who does rot practise morality teach it to another? How can a sinking man save another from drowning? The man who lives a moral life never raises the question as to how to serve the world, for he is never in doubt. Mathew Arnold says of a friend :

I saw him sensitive in frame,
I knew his spirits low,
And wished him health, success, and fame—
I do not wish it now.
For these are all their own reward,
And leave no good behind :
They try us—oftenest make us hard,
Less modest, pure, and kind.

Time was when Arnold wished his friend health, success and fame. But he did not so wish now, because his friend's happiness or misery did not depend on their presence or absence; he, therefore, only wished that his morality might ever endure. Emerson says, "Adversity is the prosperity of the great." Both the money and the fame belonging to the base are a misery to them and to the world.[1]

1. Here follows an Urdu poem by Nazir in Gujarati translation.

Index